# TRAIN
## OF THE SKIES

ISLA KAY

CALGARY, CANADA

## KAY PRESS

2021

Author: Isla Kay

Illustrator: Sergey Avdeev

Designer: Kristen Thorley

Dedicated to William,
Oliver, & Henry

William, Oliver, and Henry knew a lot about trains.
One day, they came up with an outstanding idea:
to make a train that could FLY.

Henry used his blue crayon to draw up the blueprints, and
Oliver and William used lego to make the train model.
"It's just like our train set!" said William.
It was. Except this train would be HUGE.

"But how do we build it?" Henry asked.
"With a 3D printer, don't you know!" said Oliver.

"This part fits here," said William, assembling the pieces.
"And this part goes here!" said Oliver.
"Needs more blue," said Henry.

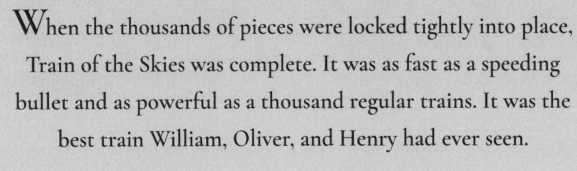

When the thousands of pieces were locked tightly into place, Train of the Skies was complete. It was as fast as a speeding bullet and as powerful as a thousand regular trains. It was the best train William, Oliver, and Henry had ever seen.

"Will it really fly?" Oliver wondered.
"Only one way to find out," said Henry.
"I can't wait to fly it," said William.
"No, I'm going to fly it!" said Oliver.
"We'll all fly it together," they decided.

No one had ever flown a train before. A senior pilot named
Tommy Jetson would teach the boys how to fly the train.

"Who here knows how to fly?" asked Tommy.
"I've flown a kite," said Oliver.
"So have I!" said William.
"I skated so fast once, I almost flew," said Henry.

"First thing's first..." Tommy began.
"If you want a cookie, press this button."
"Yum," said William, taking a bite.

They spent all day learning the hundreds of buttons
and levers.

Finally... it was time to fly.

It was a beautiful sunny morning in the city of Calaway as Train of the Skies picked up speed on the train track, its propeller turning around and around.

"It's a special day!" said Grammy Peggy.

"Be safe!" said Grandpa Doug.

"Take care!" said Grandma Brenda.

"Buckle up!" said Grandpa Steve.

Train of the Skies went faster and faster
until it shot up into the bright blue sky.
"Whoaaa!" said the boys, hanging on to
their hats. The passengers cheered.

"We have lift off!"
William announced over the speaker.

High above, a tunnel of white clouds had formed around them until
they couldn't see a thing.

"Oh no!" said Oliver.

"Ahhhhh!" said William. "I can't see! Railroad disaster!"

They steered Train of the Skies through the foggy white tunnel.

"How are we supposed to know where we're going?" Oliver worried.

"Going to the donut car," said Henry. "See ya!"

Train of the Skies had separate cars for each dessert.

There was a donut car that had 100 flavors of donuts in glass cases, an ice cream car designed like a soda shop that was kept as cool as the North Pole, and a bakery car that sold only blue cupcakes.

"Hey Henry, bring us back two sprinkle donuts," said Oliver.

"Okay," said Henry. "Two sprinkle donuts coming up."

But trouble lay ahead.

As Train of the Skies rose higher and higher, dark blue and purple clouds rumbled with thunder outside.

"Crrrrack!" a lightning bolt pierced the sky with a stripe of white light.

William took the radio: "Ladies and gentlemen, we're experiencing some turbulence, if you could please put your marshmallow hats on."

Henry walked carefully back to the cockpit, almost losing his donuts.

Oliver tried to steer away from the storm, but it was too close – they would have to fly through it.

"Hold on to your marshmallow hats!" William told the passengers over the radio.
The train shook from side to side, up and down, like they were on a trampoline.

Oliver held the throttle, tightly. "Whoaaa," he said, as the train shook every which way.
"BOOM!" went the lightning.

The donuts and cupcakes went flying!

After their snack, the boys were full of energy. They regained control of the train, and made it back to calm blue skies.

"Look," said Oliver, "a rainbow!"

They flew right through the middle of the beautiful arc of blue, green, purple, red, orange, and yellow as they traversed the Rocky Road Mountains.

"Hey, I see the cabin!" said Henry.
Over Inthemirror Lake, they saw their cabin from far above.

On the horizon, far away, a blinking green light flashed.

"Hey, what's that?" asked Oliver.

"Aliens!" the boys screamed.

"MEEP MOORK," the aliens blasted from their supersonic speakers.

"What does it mean?" asked William.

"Ummm...." said Henry. "I know! Use the decoder."

Oliver typed in the words. "It means: NICE_FLYING_TRAIN!"

Just then, the flying saucer disappeared as quickly
as it had appeared in a flash of green light.

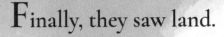

Finally, they saw land.
The beautiful island of Wahaii was covered in green palm trees and
white sand beaches. The island volcano was usually quiet…
but not today.

"Uh oh!" said William. "The volcano is erupting!"
Hot lava was gushing into the sky and they were heading right into it.
The sizzling heat was almost melting Henry's ice cream cone.
"Quick!" said William. "We need elevation. Pull up!"

The flying train shot up like a rocket just as lava reached the caboose.
"Good work, boys," said Henry.

The train landed on the tracks at Kamai'maia Train Station
as the sun set into the beautiful Wahaii ocean.
"We did it!" the boys threw off their hats.
"To the best brothers in the world!" The crowd applauded.
Their father was proud.
"Way to go, boys!" he high-fived them.

A luau had been prepared with pizza,
fries, and milkshakes. Their mother cut them
each a piece of train cake.

That night, they fell fast asleep as soon as their heads hit their marshmallow pillows.

The next morning, Henry woke up with excitement.

"I had a dream!" he said, his eyes open wide.

"It's never been done before, but it just might work..."

"Oh man!" said William. "I had the same dream!"

"We could fly to galaxies far, far away!" said Oliver.

"We could visit our alien friends!" said William

"Boys," their mother called. "Time for pancakes!"

"Shh..." said Henry. "It's a secret."

The three boys shook on it, then went downstairs in their pyjamas.

"What are you boys giggling about?" their mother asked.

"Nothing!" They smiled as they ate their pancakes.

The End!

CPSIA information can be obtained
at www.ICGtesting.com
Printed in the USA
BVRC102307281121
622743BV00001B/4